CAMDEN TOWN & KENTISH TOWN THEN & NOW

IN COLOUR

MARIANNE COLLOMS & DICK WEINDLING

The History Press

First published in 2012

The History Press
The Mill, Brimscombe Port
Stroud, Gloucestershire, GL5 2QG
www.thehistorypress.co.uk

British Library Cataloguing in Publication Data.
A catalogue record for this book is available from the British Library.

ISBN 978 0 7524 7467 0

Typesetting and origination by The History Press
Printed in Turkey.

CONTENTS

ACKNOWLEDGEMENTS

The authors would like to thank the staff of the Camden Local Studies and Archives Centre for their continuing help and co-operation. Special thanks are due Roger Crocombe for his time and his excellent photographs.

Every effort has been made to contact the owners of the images reproduced in this book. All illustrations are copyright and reproduced with the kind permission of the following:

The London Borough of Camden: Kentish Town by Grimm p.6; Inwood Place p.11; Bedford Theatre p.17; Cobden statue p.20; Rowney factory p.23; Bull & Gate p.66; Beddalls p.77; Daniels p.79; Salmon & Gluckstein p.80; Camden Lock p.86; Brown's dairy p.91; Chalk Farm bridge p.95.

Roger Crocombe: photographs, p.7, p.24, p.27, p.36, p.39, p.51, p.53, p.54, p.57, p.60, p.63, p.65, p.75, p.87, p.90, p.93.

The Sainsbury Archive, Museum of London Docklands, Kentish Town Road p.82.

All other illustrations and photographs copyright of Marianne Colloms and Dick Weindling.

ABOUT THE AUTHORS

Marianne Colloms has co-authored a number of articles and books on the history of Camden, in particular Hampstead, Kilburn, Camden and Kentish Towns. She is also a partner in a long established design consultancy.

Dick Weindling was previously head of Educational Management at the National Foundation for Educational Research (NFER) and then a freelance educational researcher. Specialising in the work of new head teachers he wrote several education books. He has now retired and works on history projects with his writing colleague Marianne Colloms.

INTRODUCTION

This book shows the changing face of an area of north London. Originally the adjacent districts of Kentish Town and Camden Town lay in the parish, later the borough of St Pancras. Today this forms part of the borough of Camden. Kentish and Camden Towns developed along two major routes that led north from central London to the villages of Hampstead and Highgate. The road to Highgate passed by the parish church of St Pancras. The earliest settlement in the area was established nearby, on the banks of the Fleet River. The local fields were primarily meadowland and a large number of public houses were built on the main roads.

A second group of houses developed further north, near the present junction of Royal College Street and Kentish Town Road. This became the village of Kentish Town. 'Camden Town' did not exist until Lord Camden obtained a 1791 Act of Parliament to grant building leases for his property east of Camden High Street. Other landowners soon followed his example and started to develop their properties.

As the nineteenth century progressed, builders created a network of residential streets, lined with terraced houses or semi-detached villas. The main roads became prime shopping areas, supplying most of the needs of local householders. The Regent's Canal opened in 1820 and the London and Birmingham Railway began running trains through Camden Town to their terminus at Euston in 1837. Two more railway companies laid tracks across the fields of Kentish Town in the 1850s and 1860s. On the roads, horse buses were joined by trams and later replaced by motor and trolley buses. Industry was drawn to the streets near the railway lines and canal, providing much local employment, as did the railways themselves. The area became a noted centre of the piano-making industry.

In the years immediately preceding the Second World War, Camden and Kentish Towns suffered a general decline. The area was polluted by soot and smoke from the trains. Many of the original family-owned houses had been converted into flats or bedsits and become run down. St Pancras, and later Camden Council, embarked on redevelopment schemes that eradicated entire neighbourhoods, replacing old properties with new accommodation largely in the form of blocks of flats. In post-war years, Irish, and later Greek-Cypriot, communities established themselves in Camden Town. Today both it and Kentish Town are busy cosmopolitan neighbourhoods. Good road, rail and tube links have helped promote their popularity as residential districts.

Old industries have gone, but disused buildings and sites along the canal and railway lines have been adapted for housing and commercial use, notably the area in and around Camden Lock. Many pubs continue to flourish, and some have become famous as live music venues. Events such as the annual 'Camden Crawl' attract even more visitors. Suggestions have been made that parts of busy Camden High Street should be closed to vehicles, at least at weekends. The markets of Camden Town have become one of the most popular tourist destinations in London, attracting millions of visitors each year.

THE JUNCTION OF ROYAL COLLEGE STREET AND KENTISH TOWN ROAD

LOOKING SOUTH DOWN Royal College Street and Kentish Town Road in 1772. This rural view of what was then the southern border of Kentish Town is by Swiss painter Samuel Hieronymus Grimm. Directions 'to Gray's Inn Lane' and 'to St Giles' are painted on the house at the road fork. The Black Horse tavern, with its swinging sign, is on the left (in the direction of Gray's Inn).

One eccentric landlady, Mrs Faulkner, was fond of a pipe of tobacco and kept a pig as a companion in her back parlour. When the Black Horse was put up for sale in 1854, the particulars noted that the trade in malt liquor was approaching £100 a month, or a substantial £7,000 in today's money.

THIS BUSY JUNCTION still divides traffic travelling south, but otherwise the site is unrecognisable. The roads were widened in the mid-1880s and old properties replaced by five-storey blocks of 'model dwellings' for working-class tenants. They were nicknamed 'Madhouse Mansions' in 1979 after squatters moved in; the squatters remained for five years. Until 1984, the white building that fronts both roads was the headquarters of Dunn and Co., men's outfitters, founded by Birmingham-born George Arthur Dunn. Orders were dispatched from here to over 100 branches. Dunn's had a branch at No. 343 Kentish Town Road: 'Mr Dunn used to come and upset his poor manager by arriving and staring at the window display'. The Black Horse pub has recently been redeveloped to provide private homes, although the pub sign remains.

ST PANCRAS OLD CHURCH, PANCRAS ROAD

THE VIEW OPPOSITE dates from the 1880s. Originally St Pancras churchyard lay south of the church, with St Giles in the Fields' burial ground to the north. Christian worship on this site may date back to Roman times. As the numbers of residents increased, so a new and much larger parish church was opened on Euston Road in 1822. The 'old church' then became the parish chapel and is shown here after partial rebuilding in 1847-8. Its isolated position in the open fields made the graveyard a target for the 'resurrection men'. In *A Tale of Two Cities*, Charles Dickens describes a grave robbery here, calling the gruesome act 'going a fishing'. John Flaxman, sculptor, and Sir John Soane, architect, are among the many eminent people buried here. A more notorious grave is that of Jonathan Wild, Thief Taker General. More curious still is the grave of Ramo Samee, who was a renowned Indian sword swallower, conjuror and juggler.

TODAY, THE EXTERIOR of the church is little altered and the burial grounds form St Pancras Gardens. In 1866-67, the Midland Railway line to St Pancras was built through the churchyard. The author Thomas Hardy, then a young trainee architect, worked on the project, and he was appalled as dismembered bodies and coffins were roughly unearthed. It influenced his poem *The Levelled Churchyard*, where he wrote: 'We late-lamented resting here, are mixed to human jam'. The Hardy tree is surrounded by tombstones rescued by Thomas during the excavation. In 2002, there were further protests when mechanical diggers removed and damaged coffins during construction of the Channel Tunnel rail link.

KENTISH TOWN ROAD, LOOKING NORTH

THE PHOTOGRAPH ON the right was taken before the
arrival of the Midland Railway. It shows the Assembly
House, the low white building at the corner of Leighton
Road, and the terraced properties of Montague Place
and Inwood Place, the latter's name clearly displayed
on a name plaque. James Frederick King lived at No. 3
Montague Place. He drew a continuous panorama of all
the houses on either side of Highgate Road, Kentish Town
Road and St Pancras Way. The three rolls are now in the
Camden Archive. Designed to show the district in around
1800, they were actually produced in the late 1840s and
the early 1850s. By 1868, the Midland Railway Station
had replaced Montague Place.

IN 1907, KENTISH Town Underground station on the Northern Line was opened. Designed by Leslie Green, his stations have a dark-red glazed terracotta façade and semi-circular windows at first-floor level. The roof was left flat, to allow for additional commercial storeys to be added. The glazed canopy (in the middle distance) on the corner of Leighton Road originally formed part of Elstree Station. It was moved to its present position in the early 1980s when Kentish Town main-line station was demolished, and shared access created with the Underground.

AMPTHILL SQUARE, OFF HAMPSTEAD ROAD

PICTURED IN AROUND 1900, this neighbourhood began building in the mid-1840s. Called 'Bedford New Town' after the landowner the Duke of Bedford, the Ampthill Square houses were built around an oval garden bisected by the cutting carrying the railway into Euston (to the left of the boys). Attempts were made to stop locomotives from smoking and annoying residents. In 1851, George Rowney, maker of artists' colours, was living at No. 2 Ampthill Square. Nearby, No. 2 Houghton Place (leading north out of Ampthill Square) was home to Charles Dickens' mistress, Ellen Ternan, and later the home of the artist Spencer Gore. The pair of semi-detached villas on the right was

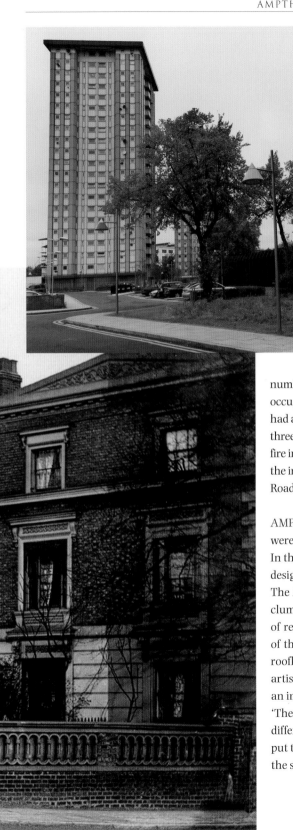

numbered 36a and 37a. In 1881, 36a was occupied by tailor Jacob Lazarus. He previously had a shop on nearby Hampstead Road, where three of his children tragically suffocated in a fire in 1866. No. 37a became the vicarage of the incumbent of St James' church, Hampstead Road, which was demolished in 1956.

AMPTHILL SQUARE AND neighbouring streets were swept away by the council in the 1960s. In their place arose the Ampthill Square estate, designed by architects Eric Lyons and Partners. The *Buildings of London* series describes 'three clumsy tower blocks', but in 2002, a majority of residents were against demolishing any of the buildings. Their distinctive coloured rooflines (red, blue and yellow) prompted local artist Frank Auerbach to paint the blocks; in an interview with John Tusa, he commented: 'There's a set of three tower-blocks with different coloured head-bands on them and I put those into a painting.' The coloured tops of the street lamps echo the theme.

13

MORNINGTON CRESCENT

ACROSS THE HAMPSTEAD Road from Ampthill Square, this photograph shows the railings and trees of the communal garden in front of the Mornington Crescent houses. Eminent residents have included artist Walter Sickert (No. 6, which has a Blue Plaque); Lord Tennyson; actress Ellen Terry; and the Rossetti family. Sickert was a member of the Camden Town Group, as was his neighbour, Spencer Gore. While lodging at No. 31, Spencer painted the view across the Crescent's gardens towards the Camden Theatre. Sickert completed many fine paintings of the interior and of performing artists at the nearby Bedford Music Hall, on Camden High Street. A series of nudes, entitled the 'Camden Town Murder', are part of the case that American crime writer Patricia Cornwell used in 2002 to name

Sickert as 'Jack the Ripper'. However, her evidence is far from conclusive and Ripper experts are not convinced.

TODAY THE HOUSES remain, but their view has been obstructed. In 1920 the Mornington Crescent garden was bought by Frederick George Minter, a builder and speculator. Campaigns were launched to preserve the space but permission was given to build on the land. The 'world's new wonder factory', the Arcadia Works, originally owned by cigarette manufacturer Carreras, opened in the autumn of 1928. Raw tobacco was delivered and cigarettes dispatched from here. The contemporary discovery of Tutankhamen's tomb inspired its extravagant Egyptian design. It was nicknamed 'the Black Cat factory' after two 7ft tall black cats which were installed at the main entrance. The company also made 'Black Cat' brand cigarettes. Described in 1936 as 'dignified and beautiful', the building was later called 'abominable' by historian Nikolaus Pevsner. Carreras moved to Basildon and sold the factory in 1959. Although some residents wanted the building demolished, the exterior was restored in 1998-9. The cats (not visible) still remain, though they are now replicas.

THE BEDFORD THEATRE, CAMDEN HIGH STREET

THE SPLENDID EXTERIOR in 1904 (opposite). It was first opened in 1861 as a music hall in the garden of the Bedford Arms, and re-building in the late 1890s transformed the Bedford into one of London's premier music halls. The interior was well recorded by Walter Sickert and other members of the Camden Town Group. Famous artistes including Marie Lloyd, Gracie Fields and Charlie Chaplin played there. Belle Elmore, the wife of Dr Crippen, also appeared. Unfortunately, she lacked talent. When Marie Lloyd spotted Belle breaking a picket line during the music-hall strike of 1907, she is supposed to have shouted, 'Let her through: she'll close the place faster than we can.' In 1929, the actor Peter Sellers – then only four years old – lived for a while with his mother Peg in rented rooms at the Bedford. Peg was performing there in a revue called *Ha!Ha!Ha!*, along with Peter's father, Bill.

BETWEEN 1933 AND 1939 the Bedford became an ABC cinema, before reverting to a theatre. It was used as a location for the 1949 film *Trottie True*, the story of a young girl's rise to fame as a music-hall star. In 1951, the year the doors finally closed, it doubled for a Dublin theatre in *The Secret People*, a film about two refugee sisters. In 1955, plans to build a library on the site were cancelled. The council then opened an adventure playground on land behind the theatre in 1963, the first full-time play centre run by a local authority. The theatre was frequently vandalised, and was demolished in 1968-69; it was replaced by commercial premises. The current Job Centre was previously an Abbey National, sited where the theatre entrance used to be. Residential accommodation (at No. 88 Arlington Road) now covers the site of the old auditorium.

THE CAMDEN THEATRE, CAMDEN HIGH STREET

THE PHOTOGRAPH BELOW dates from 1904. Originally the Royal Camden Theatre, the architect was William Sprague, who designed many of London's theatres. Advertisements appeared as building progressed, describing it as the 'handsomest', the 'grandest' and the 'most magnificent' theatre in Great Britain. Formally opened on 21 December 1900 by famous actress Ellen Terry, the Camden was certainly a luxurious and splendid venue. It could seat 3,000 people in its plush red-and-gold interior, and boasted electric lighting throughout. The first production was *Cinderella*, a pantomime that made

liberal use of local place names: the action was set in the village of 'Appy 'Ampstead, while characters included Sir Haverstock Hill and Sir Regent Spark. William Gillette's play *Sherlock Holmes* transferred to Camden Town from the Lyceum Theatre in September 1904.

IN 1909, THE theatre was renamed 'the Camden Hippodrome, home to variety', but its appeal was short-lived. In 1913 it was converted into a cinema, which closed around 1940. The BBC occupied the building from 1945 and a plaque notes that the last *Goon Show* was recorded here in April 1972. Today it has lost the statues ornamenting the roofline as well as its roof lantern but otherwise the exterior is remarkably well preserved. The building was saved from demolition in the 1970s and is now Grade II listed. As the Camden Palace (1982) and Koko (2004), it remains a popular live music venue. Numerous bands have played here, including the Rolling Stones, the Eurythmics, the Cure and, in 1983, the first UK show from a rising star known as Madonna. More recently, Kasabian, Coldplay and the Scissor Sisters have all played at Koko.

UNVEILING THE COBDEN STATUE AT MORNINGTON CRESCENT

MADE FROM SICILIAN marble by W&T Wills of Euston Road, the ceremony to unveil the statue took place on 27 June 1868. Richard Cobden, MP, was best known for his campaign to abolish the Corn Laws. Unfortunately, it proved hard to raise money for the statue and the final few pounds were still owed on the morning of the unveiling! Napoleon III was a major contributor, in recognition of Cobden having negotiated a free-trade treaty with France. Cobden's widow Catherine and their three daughters were present at the ceremony. Their host was Claude Claremont and the photo may have been taken from his house, now under the nearby tube station. The boys of the North London Collegiate School were also watching from the windows of the building on the right, as well as many of the residents in the terrace of private houses with walled front gardens beyond the school.

THE GARDENS WERE soon built over to create ground-floor shops, but the upper floors of the houses look remarkably similar today. Ellen Cobden, one of Richard's daughters, returned to live in nearby Mornington Crescent as the wife of artist Walter Sickert. In 1897, Oetzmann's cabinet factory took over the school building from the North London Collegiate. They finally moved out in 1955 and the building was redeveloped. In December 1964, publisher Victor Gollancz opened a public library on the ground floor, in vacant showrooms only recently completed for London Rediffusion, who continued to occupy the floors above. Today the building is in mixed commercial and residential use. In 1997 the Cobden statue and its hard standing were renovated at a cost of £10,000, but the railings are not part of the original installation: rather, they guard a later electricity transformer chamber.

THE ROWNEY FACTORY AT MALDEN CRESCENT

MALDEN · FACTORIES ·
MALDEN CRESCENT KENTISH TOWN N.W.
for F.W. ROWNEY ESQR
EBBETTS AND COBB ARCHITECTS
SAVOY HOUSE STRAND W·C·

ROWNEY'S LARGE FACTORY, the Malden Works, was the work of architects Ebbetts and Cobb. Built behind the houses of Malden Crescent in 1880, at a cost of nearly £20,000 (over £1 million today), the company was an important local employer. Thomas Rowney progressed from supplying artists' colours in the late eighteenth century to manufacturing them. Both Constable

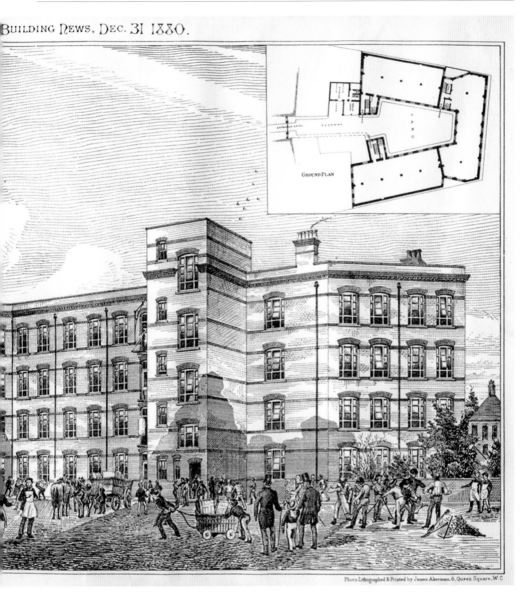

BUILDING NEWS, DEC. 31 1880.

GROUND PLAN

Photo Lithographed & Printed by James Akerman, 6, Queen Square, W.C.

and Turner used Rowney's paints. The company exhibited at the Great Exhibition of 1851, by which time it was selling a full range of artists' materials. The 1861 census shows George Rowney had moved from Ampthill Square to neighbouring Oakley Square, also in Bedford New Town. He then employed seventy-six men, and thirty-two boys and girls. The Malden Works were badly damaged by fire in 1912.

ROWNEY & CO. left Kentish Town and moved to Bracknell in 1967. It remained a family-run firm until 1969 and became Daler-Rowney in 1985. The Malden Works site was redeveloped by Camden Council as part of the Denton estate, completed in 1972.

MALDEN ROAD,
LOOKING SOUTH

THIS BUSY SHOPPING street is
pictured on the right in around 1906.
The Ponsford Arms (with roof urns
and projecting lantern) stood on
the corner of Rhyl Street. In 1857,
as building in the area was getting
underway, the recently completed pub
was put up for sale, 'decidedly in the
most favourable situation imaginable
for the early development of an
extensive, independent, and profitable
trade.' The philosopher Karl Marx
was then living nearby in Grafton
Terrace. The man in the doorway of
No. 61 is wearing a striped apron, the
trademark of a butcher. Henry Webb
and his wife Rebecca opened their shop
in the 1850s and, when her husband

died, Rebecca and son Harry continued the business. The No. 5 bus ran from Hampstead Heath to Victoria, and just out of sight in the far distance is the Rowney pencil factory.

No. 61 WAS STILL a butcher's shop in 1970, but subsequent local authority redevelopment has erased all the buildings on the right. On their site, Camden Council built a large seven-storey block, Southfleet, in 1969-75. Designed by their own architects, it forms part of a larger estate described in the *Buildings of England* series as a 'forbiddingly dense craggy group with long jutting balconies in brown brick'. Today, the No. 24 bus still links Hampstead Heath with Victoria.

MAITLAND PARK ROAD

POSTED IN 1907, the message on this postcard reads 'you will see Eidy on her bike and her friend'. Maitland Park was an enclave of comfortable villas. The block of flats replaced No. 1 Maitland Park Road (where Karl Marx moved from Grafton Terrace) in 1864. The first volume of *Das Kapital* was published while he was living here, close to the Primrose Hill home of his friend Friedrich Engels. Described by Marx's daughter as a 'veritable palace and far too expensive', in 1875 he rented a more modest terrace property up the road, No. 41 Maitland Park. Marx died there in

1883, predeceased by his wife. Both are buried in Highgate Cemetery. The Congregational chapel was used by the children from the nearby Orphan School, who nicknamed it 'Jack's Bakery' because it was so hot in the summer. Completed in 1849 at a cost of £2,681, it closed in 1946.

ALL THE MAITLAND Park houses and the chapel were demolished and their sites redeveloped by the London County Council in 1959-64. During the building work in 1963, a labourer uncovered a hoard of sixty-two gold sovereigns buried under a tree on the site. He took them to the police. A few weeks later, it was decided that the money was 'treasure trove', as it had most likely been hidden rather than abandoned. *The Times* concluded the finder 'would probably get his treasure back'. The modern block with yellow brickwork is Silverbirch Walk, built for the GLC in 1972.

CAMBRIDGE HOUSE, REGENT'S PARK

THE ADULT ORPHAN Institution moved here from Mornington Crescent. Founded in 1820, women whose fathers had been in the Navy, the Army or the Church were trained as governesses or teachers. Renamed Princess Helena College, the school left for Ealing in 1882. The building became a private residence: as Cambridge House it was home to Camden Town distiller Sir Walter Gilbey, whose household in 1901 included no less than twenty-three servants. He sold the property and auctioned the contents in 1910. The next owner was the Earl of Chesterfield, who renamed it Scudamore House.

Shortly before Christmas 1919, Major Harold Wernher (son of diamond merchant Sir Julius Wernher) moved into what was now called Someries House. Harold's wife Zia was the daughter of Grand Duke Michael, grandson of Tsar Nicholas I. The Grand Duke (once resident at Kenwood House, Hampstead) was living in neighbouring Cambridge Gate.

SOMERIES HOUSE WAS damaged by a bomb in the Second World War. It was purchased by the Royal College of Physicians and permission to demolish was given, on condition that the new building would 'harmonise' with its surroundings. (Sir) Denys Lasdun was appointed as the architect, after making it clear he would not design a building in the classical style. The College moved from Pall Mall East to Regent's Park in 1964. The Grade I listed, T-shaped building is considered to be Lasdun's most successful creation. As a link with the past, it incorporates a historic panelled room removed bodily from the old building to the new.

GOLDINGTON STREET CORNER

THIS VIEW, LOOKING towards the trees of Goldington Square, dates from about 1901. This terrace north of Platt Street was built in the late 1840s. For over thirty years, the corner premise was a butcher's shop. It had become a coffee house by 1901, advertising 'coffee and tea always ready', and 'beefsteak pudding, 4d'. This accounts for the carts; the drivers are enjoying a meal, as are their horses. The photographer had his back to the Star Tavern, which doubled, for a time, as a music hall.

An 1866 poster advertised 'W. Pennington, the Great Wizard', who during the evening promised to reveal a very curious piece of information to every single lady in the audience: nothing less than the identity of 'the gentleman she will be married to'!

THE TERRACE STILL stands, and the corner premise, with some modification, is now a private house. The houses opposite were demolished by St Pancras Council and their sites redeveloped as part of Cecil Rhodes House, a block of flats dating from 1948-50. At the far end of the terrace, a disused chapel provided a home, from 1937, for the Unity Theatre. Renowned for its productions of left-wing drama, many well-known actors appeared here, including Bill Owen, Michael Gambon, Bob Hoskins and Warren Mitchell. The theatre was gutted by a fire in 1975.

ST MICHAEL'S CHURCH, CAMDEN ROAD

ST MICHAEL'S WAS designed by Thomas Garner of Messrs Bodley and Garner. The parish was formed in 1876, and from the following February services were held in an empty shop, No. 5a Camden Road. The rooms above provided a home for the first vicar, Hampshire-born Edward

Bainbridge Penfold. Services were transferred to a temporary church on site after August 1879. The land for the church cost just under £2,500 and the foundation stone was laid in June 1880.

TODAY THE GRADE II listed church looks little altered, as plans for a tower where the tree now flourishes were never realised. To mark its 125th anniversary in 2002, the vicar again held a service in 5a Camden Road, a betting shop. The block on the left, with shops below, is Barnes House, built in 1932 by St Pancras Council. The two-storey grey building beyond the church is a large Sainsbury's supermarket (built in 1988). The designer was Nicholas Grimshaw, also responsible for the Eurostar terminus at Waterloo. The supermarket replaced a much taller building, opened in 1934, which became the main centre of operations for the ABC Bakery chain. Locals still remember the smell of baking bread, which permeated the neighbourhood until the bakery shut in 1982.

ALBERT ROAD,
PRIMROSE HILL

THE PHOTOGRAPH BELOW dates from around 1900. St Mark's church is in the distance. The
horse bus ran to Bayswater, hence the sign in the window 'to and from Whiteley's', a large
department store in Westbourne Grove. The nearest house (No. 23) was called Mymms Villa,
the first of four pairs of attractive symmetrical villas near the church. In 1871 and 1881 it
was home to (Sir) George Findlay, general manager of the London North Western Railway,
with its London terminus at Euston. A long-term occupant of No. 16, opposite St Mark's, was

piano-maker John Brinsmead, who had a factory in Kentish Town. In 1901, James Marix, an American journalist, was at No. 21. Along with two other men, Marix had previously been charged with extorting money by threatening to print a false libel. The case went to court in 1889 but eventually the jury was discharged, having failed to reach a verdict.

ALBERT ROAD WAS renamed Prince Albert Road in 1937. The trees on the right are in London Zoo, which had an entry gate opposite these houses (since closed). The proximity of the Zoological Gardens prompted comment from the vicar of St Mark's in 1959: 'This is a pagan district. Many people simply regard St Mark's as a bus stop for the zoo'! Mymms Villa was demolished in the 1960s and replaced by the large red brick block of flats. The Regent's Canal runs along the zoo side of the road, making a sharp turn at St Mark's to head towards Camden Town lock. A branch that went to the Cumberland Market, north of Euston Road, has been infilled, and all that remains is the small Cumberland basin opposite the church. There is mooring for a few boats and there has been a floating restaurant here since 1963.

REGENT'S PARK ROAD

ALL THESE HOUSES were probably the
work of architect Henry Bassett. The large
fifteen-room house with Italianate style
twin towers stood at the junction with
Gloucester Avenue. It took just two weeks
to dismiss, in 1905, the proposal that the
house be demolished and the site used for
workmen's housing for those displaced
by railway extensions near Euston. The
suggestion may have had something to do
with the fact that the occupant at the time,
Carl Edward Grasemann, was chief goods
manager of the rail company concerned!
The house eventually succumbed in 1927,
and the foundation stone of Cecil Sharp
House was laid in June 1929. The villas
on the right survived until 1970-71, but
despite a spirited battle to save them, they
were demolished and replaced by flats.

CECIL SHARP HOUSE opened on Whit Sunday, 1931. Designed by H.M. Fletcher for what became the English Folk Dance and Song Society, the building was named for Cecil Sharp (who died in 1924). As a result of his recordings of the music and dances of English folklore, much survived that would otherwise have been lost. In addition to concerts and recitals, it was originally intended to create an open-air theatre in the space in front of the building. Repair of bomb damage following the Second World War included adding a storey; in the main hall, a massive mural, executed on eleven canvases, was also commissioned. The artist was Ivon Hitchens. Unveiled in 1954, it depicts four well-known English country dances in a woodland setting. Prompted by dwindling interest in folk music, the Society survived a 1980s attempt to sell off the listed Grade II property. Today Cecil Sharp House is home to the National Folk Music and Dance Archive.

REGENT'S PARK ROAD CONTINUED

THIS IMPOSING TERRACE, Nos 72 to 94 Regent's Park Road, was originally called Regent's Park Gardens. The census reveals some interesting occupants: there was Thomas George Mackinlay (1861), piano maker, music publisher, and a pioneer photographer. Frederick Whinney was at

No. 90 for many years. He helped establish the accountancy profession, his firm being the oldest partnership later absorbed by Ernst and Young. William Broomfield, part-owner of *Sporting Life*, was at No. 78 in 1911. The nearest property, No. 72, had more notorious connections: in 1901, this was the Drouet Institute for the Deaf, where Dr Crippen worked for a few years. One work colleague was a young typist named Ethel le Neve, who became Crippen's mistress. Crippen mainly diagnosed from letters and sent out mail-order cures, including curative plasters to stick behind the ear! The firm was exposed as a sham by *Truth* magazine.

THE TERRACE AND adjoining properties were demolished in 1963 and replaced by the Oldfield Estate. 'Oldfield' was the name of the purchaser of the land when it was sold for building back in 1840.

No. 39
HILLDROP CRESCENT

IN 1910, DR Hawley Harvey Crippen was convicted of murdering his wife Cora at their home, No. 39 Hilldrop Crescent. Cora had bullied her meek husband and spent well beyond their income, partly to bolster her unsuccessful music-hall career as singer 'Belle Elmore'. It was believed that Crippen poisoned Cora and buried her in the cellar. With his mistress Ethel le Neve, who was disguised as a young man, Crippen fled to Canada aboard the SS *Montrose*. But the suspicious captain alerted the police by wireless, and the couple were arrested before landing. An Old Bailey jury convicted Crippen; he was executed on 23 November 1910. Ethel was acquitted. She later married, had a family and died in 1967. The man standing on the steps is the next occupant, Sandy McNab.

AFTER THE TRIAL and the huge publicity which surrounded it, the house was bought by the Scottish music-hall artist Sandy McNab, who turned it into a Crippen museum. But he was forced to abandon the scheme after neighbours complained. In 1914 Sandy, whose real name was Adam Arthur, was sentenced to two years' hard labour for an offence involving a thirteen-year old girl. The house was bombed in the Second World War and the site demolished. In 2007, research at Michigan State University showed that DNA from the remains found in the cellar did not match those of Cora's relatives. This has raised questions about who was buried in the cellar – and, by implication, about Crippen's guilt. The present flats, 'Margaret Bondfield House', were named after the first British female MP to become a Cabinet Minister; Margaret Bondfield took her seat in 1929.

A CAMDEN TOWN STAMPEDE

SHORTLY AFTER 10 P.M. on the 9 June 1857,
a fire broke out in the warehouses of Pickford's
the carriers, by the Regent's Canal at Camden
Town. Brave volunteers released the horses stabled
in vaults below the warehouse. This dramatic
picture looks north up Oval Road from Collard's
circular piano factory (right), at the corner with
Gloucester Crescent. The horses stampeded into
the surrounding streets. Some were driven towards
Highgate and almost trampled a startled police
inspector on his way to fight the fire. Poultry, goats
and pigs perished in the flames – but only one
bad-tempered horse, named 'the Manhunter', died:
he wouldn't allow anyone to lead him out. At one
point, the flames were 'overlapping' the roof of the
Stanhope Arms immediately opposite Pickford's
gates. Part of its name can be seen below the
flag-staff. The public house survived but Pickford's
premises were completely destroyed.

LOOKING NORTH UP Oval Road today, a short terrace is all that has survived further on from
Gloucester Crescent. When Pickford's premises were rebuilt, new stables were provided off site
in Gloucester Avenue, reached by a tunnel under the railway lines. Collard originally had two
premises in the street: the one by the railway, shown in the 1857 image, has been demolished
but, across the road, the factory still stands. Sadly the lion has long disappeared from its
remodelled entrance. Camden Town was a centre for the piano-making industry and this was
the main Collard factory. The nearby canal and railway used to transport both raw materials
and completed instruments. Designed by Thomas and William Piper in 1852, the factory
had twenty-two sides to maximise light and floor space. It was later occupied by publishers
Duckworth and Virago.

A RAILWAY CRASH IN KENTISH TOWN

ON THE EVENING of 2 September 1861, an excursion train returning from Kew hit an empty ballast train, which was standing on a bridge about 450 yards south of Gospel Oak station. Nineteen-year-old Henry Raynor, a porter at the station, covered for the signal man during meal breaks. Henry allowed the passenger train through without making sure that the line was empty. The resulting crash had devastating consequences: the excursion train engine (plus several carriages) fell on one side of the embankment, and trucks from the ballast train on the other: 16 people died and over 300 were injured, 20 seriously. The jurors at the inquest had the gruesome task of viewing the bodies of the deceased. Raynor was committed for trial for manslaughter, but

the inquest criticised the railway company for using inexperienced staff. He was acquitted that October and remained in railway employment for the rest of his life, as a clerk.

THE CRASH OCCURRED roughly where the viaduct intersected Carker's Lane, which led west off Highgate Road to Gospel Oak. At this point the railway crossed open ground. One witness, who later gave evidence at the inquest, was labourer Thomas Simpson, who was lying in a field near the embankment behind Carlton Road (now Grafton Road), smoking his pipe, when the crash occurred. Today Carker's Lane is a short *cul de sac*, eroded by later railway building, while the railway viaduct is hemmed in on both sides by trading estates or houses. This partially rebuilt bridge is very near to the accident and is the closest span accessible to the public. It stands at the end of Arctic Street off Spring Place and shows several of the architectural details in the etching. The space under the bridge is now used as a garage for car repairs.

45

ST PANCRAS PUBLIC BATHS

ST PANCRAS PUBLIC Baths, with its roof lantern, was designed by Thomas Aldwinkle. The site cost £18,000 and the building just under £80,000. The water was drawn from artesian wells. Opened in October 1901, Mr Pearce, the building superintendent, took 'the first plunge'. At the time, many homes lacked proper washing facilities. So, in addition to four swimming pools, this building also provided residents with personal 'slipper' baths plus fifty washing sinks with mangles, irons and drying horses. Each facility had a separate entrance with their names above the door: men's first and second class (baths), ladies (baths), public hall and public washhouse. One pool was converted into a public-entertainment space during the winter months. The job of baths

superintendent included on-site accommodation; in 1911, the superintendent was Edward Akroyd, whose wife Mary was the matron. Her role included running a crèche for mothers doing their laundry.

DESPITE POST-SECOND World War improvements, facilities at the baths deteriorated. Suggestions were made to convert part of the Grade II listed building into flats. Poor conditions forced closure in 2007 and Camden Council embarked on an ambitious restoration and updating programme that cost an estimated £25 million. The Baths re-opened to the public in 2010 and the building now offers all the facilities of a modern sports centre. Exterior details such as the lettering, the terracotta frieze at first-floor level and figures, including saints, bearded river gods and devils, have been carefully restored. Una House, the flats on the right, were built by St Pancras Council in 1922 and renovated in 2003. The local press noted the name 'Una' was taken from Spencer's *Faerie Queen*, where she is the 'embodiment of truth'.

ST PANCRAS TOWN HALL AND INFIRMARY

A LATE VICTORIAN view (right) of St Pancras Town Hall, St Pancras Way; the Town Hall is the building on the left. The first Town Hall opened here in 1847, but this frontage dates from 1874-5. The inquest into the 1861 Kentish Town rail crash was held in a large hall in the building. The new parish workhouse, which took in sick and destitute residents, opened in 1809 on land immediately behind and to the left of the Town Hall. Workhouses were unpleasant places: inmates worked hard for no wages, couples were separated, and

family contact was kept to a minimum. As the population increased, so the complex of workhouse buildings were rebuilt and expanded, and in 1885 the bay-windowed block to the right of the town hall was built as an infirmary to accommodate 400 chronically ill and elderly patients.

IN 1874, A plea was made for a 'Town Hall worthy of the great Parish of St Pancras', but no action was taken. Designed to accommodate thirty staff, by 1924 numbers had risen to 110, with eighteen clerks in one room alone! Locals had to wait until 1937 for a new Town Hall to open on Euston Road. It cost £250,000 and is currently used by the borough of Camden. The infirmary is now part of St Pancras Hospital, which also occupies some of the old workhouse buildings. When the old Town Hall was demolished, its site was absorbed into the hospital's grounds.

THE BOYS' HOME,
REGENT'S PARK ROAD

IN 1858, THE Boys' Home for the 'training and maintenance of destitute boys not convicted
of crime' opened at 44 Euston Road. They moved to Nos 115-117 Regent's Park Road in 1865,
when No. 44 was demolished, another casualty of the Midland Railway's extension to St Pancras.
Frederick Maurice, one of the founders of the Working Men's College in Camden Town, was an
early supporter. Every boy was carefully vetted. As well as learning a trade such as tailoring, bakery,

The Boys' Home, Regent's Park Road, N.W.

carpentry and printing, they raised funds by selling the goods they produced. Lessons included the basic 'Three Rs', plus some history, geography, drawing and singing. There was also an excellent band. It led the boys each Wednesday to play football on Primrose Hill and was hired out for garden parties and events at the zoo.

THE 1911 CENSUS lists 135 boys at the Home, the majority of them London-born and the youngest just eight years old. After the Second World War, the Home could not raise the necessary funds to move to the country and was closed down in 1920. During its sixty-year life, it had provided an education and training for hundreds of boys. When they left, they were given some money and a suit of clothes and generally found jobs. One report noted, 'the attachment of old boys to their school is remarkable.' Today, the exterior of the main building has survived well, and with some modifications it is split between residential and commercial premises. The tower blocks in the background on Adelaide Road were part of a mixed private and council redevelopment plan begun in 1965.

THE WORKING MEN'S COLLEGE, CROWNDALE ROAD

THE WORKING MEN'S College soon after opening in Camden Town, in 1906 (below). The date of '1854' is misleading, as it actually refers to the original foundation in Red Lion Square.

Working Men's College, Crowndale Road, N.W.

Established by F.D. Maurice, Charles Kingsley, and other members of the Christian Socialists, this was a pioneering establishment for adult education that sought to impart knowledge, not simply vocational skills. This building was designed by W.D. Caroe; the land cost £6,600 and the red-brick buildings cost a further £25,500. Facilities included thirty classrooms, laboratories, a music room and gymnasium to serve some 1,000 students. The principal described the building as 'not showy, but good, suitable for work, and admirable for the purpose for which it was designed.' More rooms were added in the 1930s.

THE GRADE II listed college is another building that has survived the passing of the years remarkably well. Women were admitted for the first time in 1960, and this adult education college currently caters for about 5,000 students. George Orwell, Vaughan Williams and Seamus Heaney are among many eminent persons who have taught at the college.

CAMDEN HIGH STREET

THIS IMAGE LOOKS north up
Camden High Street, *c*. 1904. In the
background, the shop awnings and
flag mark the site of the extensive
premises of Bowman Brothers,
Camden Town's leading store. In
1864, brothers Thomas and Robert
Bowman opened an upholstery
business in Camden Town. The firm
rapidly expanded, surviving a fire
in 1893, to occupy Nos 112 to 138
Camden High Street. The shop offered
an extensive range of furniture and
household goods, aiming to supply
'every household requisite'. In 1900,
the company anticipated mass
migration to South Africa following
the relief of Mafeking, and advertised
'gigantic preparations for the complete
furnishing of homes'. The Dalziel
brothers moved into No. 110 (with
the triangular pediment) in 1857, and
established the Camden Press.

As printers, engravers and publishers, they ran one of England's most successful wood engraving businesses.

THIS PART OF Camden High Street lies south of today's main tourist shopping area, centred on Camden Lock. A surprising number of the buildings have survived with few alterations, but the businesses are very different. The Camden Head is the one constant and has recently reverted to using its original name. Bowman's closed in the 1980s but the frontage, rebuilt after the fire, still retains several attractive mosaic inlays above the new shop fronts. These advertise departments in the original store, and include a Viking boat and a railway engine.

PARKWAY

PARKWAY WAS ORIGINALLY called Park Street. The photograph below, taken in around 1924, looks south. The first premises on the left, Nos 110-112, was built in 1904 and has carved initials over the door; it was occupied by Benjamin Barling & Sons, the famous pipe makers. The Dublin Castle, a popular pub, was a few doors away. This became one of Camden Town's main commercial streets. A resident recalled the street after the First World War: 'It was full of shops. By eight in the morning the shop boy was cleaning the windows and polishing the outside brasses, ready to open at nine and close twelve hours later. Fenn's the grocer was a cut above the others, wrapping all purchases in brown paper, while most used newspaper.'

The English Jersey Breeders Dairies were at Nos 29-31. 'They sold off their skimmed milk. You had to be there between six and seven in the morning and you could buy a pennyworth.'

RENAMED PARKWAY IN 1937, traffic is now one way, towards Camden High Street. Barlings continued trading until 1970. Many of the upper storeys are basically unchanged and the street is still lined with businesses. Recently restaurants have taken over many of the premises, including Palmer's pet shop, which once sold monkeys and talking parrots. Palmer's young daughter 'used to sit outside the shop with a large snake coiled round her.' The Dublin Castle (painted red) is still selling pints and is one of the venues that make Camden Town famous for live music. Numerous bands have played here, including the very successful Madness, who started here in the late 1970s. Until her recent death, the pub was a favourite of Amy Winehouse. She performed at the pub during the 2007 Camden Crawl, an annual event that aims to showcase up-and-coming talent alongside established artists.

INVERNESS STREET

WELLINGTON STREET WAS renamed Inverness Street in 1937. The photograph on the right predates the First World War, with Teetgen, tea merchants, on the corner with the High Street. House building here began at the time of Waterloo, which probably explains the original name. This has long been a market street; stall holders would stay open late into Saturday evening and sell off any remaining goods at knock-down prices. Damaged fruit was thrown under the stalls, and at the end of trading local children were allowed to scavenge for what they could find. A woman sat in a hut at the corner with Camden High Street in the 1920s: 'She controlled the money in the greengrocery and fruit stalls there. They called out how much for her to take. None of the staff ever got at the money.'

THIS WAS ANOTHER Camden Town location used in the film *Trottie True*, which placed her father's business here. In the 1960s, Reggie's junk stall, at the junction of Inverness Street and Arlington Road, was a source of great 'bargains', from books and clothes to household and electrical goods. Another stall displayed a rubbery, processed pink cat food in a big block, which was cut and sold by weight. Today Inverness Street is on the main route to Camden Lock and the market still flourishes. The produce on sale has adapted to the times, with many traders catering for tourists by selling clothes and accessories. But the fruit and vegetable stalls still do a good trade, with some stall-holders using the old coster-style barrows to move their produce. These wheeled barrows were practical and also allowed traders to keep on the move in the days before licensed pitches.

CAMDEN HIGH STREET

TEETGEN'S DELIVERY CART stands outside their shop at the corner with Inverness Street (right). In 1912, Eliza Mary Barrow, the lessee of the Buck's Head pub (the tall building behind bus), was murdered by Frederick Henry Seddon. The motive was theft: Eliza gave Frederick control over her business affairs in return for a small annuity and the promise she could live rent-free in Seddon's home in Tollington Park, Islington. At the trial it was noted that brewers Truman Hanbury paid rent for the Buck's Head using an open cheque that could be cashed at a bank. The Seddons stole the money. Frederick was found guilty of poisoning Eliza, using arsenic dissolved from fly papers, but Mrs Seddon was acquitted. The talented barrister Marshall Hall defended Seddon, but Seddon's arrogant manner when giving evidence probably helped convict him. He was hanged on 18 April 1912.

TODAY THE TERRACE south of Buck Street has been demolished and the open-air Camden Market occupies their site. The Buck's Head, painted red and minus its corner sign, still stands at the corner of Buck Street and remains a popular drinking place for visitors. The shops north of the pub form part of the vibrant shopping strip along the main road leading to Camden Lock, and are known for their large advertising signs and colourful frontages. Camden Market was under threat of redevelopment but has been reprieved, although its future is still uncertain.

REGENT'S PARK ROAD

JOSEPH JUPP'S BUTCHERS shop was at No. 158 Regent's Park Road. Pictured below in around 1910, this was another busy shopping street, serving Primrose Hill and Regent's Park. Assistants were able to serve from the open front window. Customers expected same-day delivery – and judging by the number of carts, Jupp's was a substantial business. Mr Jupp is standing outside, his sharpening steel hanging from his belt. Traders often lived over their shops: you can see Mrs Jupp at a first-floor window, holding the couple's youngest child. It was common for butchers to hang fresh produce outside their shop, but this lavish display was probably created for the photograph. Some, but not Jupp, had a slaughterhouse behind their premises. The sender of the card, probably the young man marked with an 'x' in the photograph, asked that it be given 'to Ernie'. By 1911 the Jupps had left Primrose Hill for Chiswick.

TODAY No. 158 is a clothes shop (with awning) next to the premises painted red. Commerce still flourishes, but – as with so many other shopping parades in Camden and Kentish Towns – businesses like the Jupp's have largely given way to estate agents, gift shops and restaurants. While No. 158 remained a butcher's shop until the 1970s, the shop next door lasted even longer: shown as selling household wares in around 1910, it continued in the same trade under various owners, before finally closing in 2010. Over Christmas 1964, a group of young men who'd been celebrating tried to gatecrash a party at No. 170. They failed to get in and smashed the widows of the flat using milk bottles from a nearby dairy. The dairyman, Mr Griffiths, was stabbed, as was an occupant of the flat, Michael Munnelly, who died. Frederick Bishop, aged eighteen, was convinced of his murder.

No. 38 Chalcot Road

DESPITE JUPP'S BEING just a few minutes walk away, Primrose Hill residents could also buy their meat from Turner's, on the corner of Fitzroy Road and St George's (now No. 38 Chalcot) Road. The view opposite reveals another extravagant display of meat. In 1905, the sender of this card was lodging with the gentleman in the white apron. He was probably the owner, William Robert Turner, whose two sons – who also worked in the business – are pictured standing in the doorway. William had set up shop by 1871, and after he died, in 1922, the butcher's continued trading, with son Frederick taking over the business.

TODAY THE BUILDING has lost its attractive roofline detail but the shop front remains. It was home to Bentley Acoustic Co. from the early 1950s to mid-1970s, selling valves, mostly by mail order. The current business is Fonthill Pottery but the name 'Turner' and the trade of 'butcher' has recently re-emerged, as the paint obscuring the original sign has worn off the tiles.

BULL & GATE, KENTISH TOWN ROAD

PICTURED IN 1904, one unlikely explanation for the pub's name is a corruption of 'Boulogne Gate'. This was one of eleven licensed premises in Kentish Town in 1721. Its gardens were a popular resort, and as late as 1861 the landlord, George Garratt, was able to look across

open fields to the viaduct, where the excursion train had been derailed. He was the licensee for over twenty-five years. The pub was rebuilt in 1871, and three years later: 'It partakes no longer of its original quiet character. A splendid modern gin-palace now monopolises the space, and the scene is composed of departing and returning omnibuses'. The pub, as this suggests, stood at the end of a bus route.

A bull-and-gate relief was added over the main door and the rebuilding date set in the semi-circular plaque high up the fascia. The large ornamental lights were probably added in the 1890s.

TODAY THE GRADE II listed building has lost its lamps as well as some interesting exterior details from the roofline and curved corner. But inside, many original features have survived. In the early 1980s the pub was home to convivial theatrical presentations but music took over, and the old laundry is currently the entry to the 'Venue'. Many of the British jazz and blues bands regularly played here during the 1960s and '70s and the Bull and Gate has continued to be a vibrant part of the Camden music scene. It hosted early performances by Nirvana, Blur, Manic Street Preachers and Coldplay. The pub was up for sale in November 2011, for £2.7 million. Just a few doors away you will find another famous music venue in a converted cinema: The Forum, which replaced the Town and Country Club in 1992.

THE ASSEMBLY HOUSE

ONE OF THE oldest drinking places in the area, the Assembly House was
a coaching inn, originally set back from the main road. In 1725, Robert
Wright enjoyed a successful convalescence nearby, his cure including a
daily walk to the tavern to have breakfast. The grateful invalid donated an
oval table to the Assembly House. This stood outside near the tree pictured
here, which was damaged during a severe storm in 1849: 'lightening struck
a remarkably fine old elm. Some of the larger limbs nearly fell on a man
who was passing.' The landlord in around 1783 was Thomas Wood, who
advertised his extensive garden (stretching back towards today's Leighton
Road), with its skittle and 'trap-ball' ground. Wood was later tried and
acquitted of highway robbery, but allegedly died insane in 1787, after being
confined in Newgate Prison. The Assembly House was used for auctions and
meetings, and was rebuilt in 1853.

THE PRESENT BUILDING is yet another rebuild, by Kentish Town architects
Thorpe and Furniss, and dates from 1898. On the side elevation in Leighton
Road is a statue of a small boy, holding the date. Grade II listed, the building
has superb glass and ironwork, and a well-preserved Victorian interior.

Sadly Mr Wright's table, which was taken inside the building, has disappeared. The interior of the pub featured as the local 'boozer' in the 1971 film *Villain*, starring Richard Burton as a ruthless gang leader. Liz Taylor visited the location and a publicity shot showed her pulling pints behind the bar.

THE CASTLE INN,
KENTISH TOWN ROAD

THE CASTLE INN (another very old Kentish Town pub, close to the junction of Royal College Street and Kentish Town Road) in around 1800. Patronised by Londoners in search of tea and amusements, its gardens bordered the Fleet River, crossed by a drawbridge to allow visitors to enter from the fields towards Hampstead. 'The wife took her tea, while the husband indulged in his clean straw pipe and ale. The children were regaled with biscuits, or shrimps.' Concerts were held in the upstairs rooms. An 1833 handbill advertised Mr Herbert, a 'living model', who posed

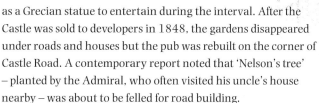

as a Grecian statue to entertain during the interval. After the Castle was sold to developers in 1848, the gardens disappeared under roads and houses but the pub was rebuilt on the corner of Castle Road. A contemporary report noted that 'Nelson's tree' – planted by the Admiral, who often visited his uncle's house nearby – was about to be felled for road building.

THE CASTLE, DESCRIBED soon after rebuilding as a 'splendid gin palace', is still open for business. Currently called Heroes, it has become a live music venue. The red-brick building next door was South Kentish Town tube station, which opened in 1907. It shut in 1924 but proved valuable as an air-raid shelter during the Second World War. John Betjeman broadcast a story about 'South Kentish Town' in 1951. Basil Green accidentally gets off at the closed station, to be rescued several hours later by railway staff. Apparently, this was inspired by a true incident shortly after the station shut. The lower floor of the station has been converted into commercial premises but the distinctive arched windows at first-floor level remain. Back in 1924, low passenger numbers contributed to its closing, but in 2011, the reverse was true, and the suggestion was made to reopen the station, to help ease congestion.

THE BRECKNOCK ARMS, CAMDEN ROAD

THE CARD BELOW was postmarked 1905. The Brecknock Arms was another pub that once had an attractive tea garden. Soon after dawn on 1 July 1843, the field behind was the scene of a duel – allegedly the last fought in London. Lieutenant Munro and Colonel Fawcett had married two sisters. At the time of the duel Munro was living in Camden Town, in the Albany Street Barracks. Munro issued a challenge to fight when Fawcett criticised the way in which his affairs had been handled by Munro during Fawcett's army service in China. Munro shot and badly wounded

his brother-in-law. The Brecknock Arms staff refused to look after Fawcett, who was carried on a shutter to the Camden Arms in Randolph Street. Before he died two days later, Fawcett said he regretted accepting the challenge. After escaping abroad, Munro returned to face trial. He was convicted of murder, but his sentence was commuted to a year's imprisonment.

THE PUB WAS put up for sale in 1862, when turnover approached £500 a month (equivalent to about £34,000 today). Sales were boosted by the absence of local competition and proximity to the Metropolitan Cattle Market on York Road, which provided a 'good return on market days in dinners and wines.' The Brecknock Arms is now The Unicorn, yet another music venue. Traces of original signage are visible underneath flaking paintwork at roof level. The modern blue building across the road from the pub replaced a low, single-storey shop, and is in mixed commercial and residential use. Recently, the Camden Arms, where the wounded man took his last breath, has changed its name to The Colonel Fawcett.

THE ADELAIDE,
CHALK FARM ROAD

IN 1842, DEVELOPER William Wynn asked Eton College (who owned the land) to support his application for a license, and the Adelaide Tavern was named after Queen Adelaide, wife of William IV. When put up for sale in 1879, the Tavern was described as 'cheerfully situated', but the details advised that after some thirty years under one landlord, the 'new era' of drinkers

would expect the facilities to be upgraded: 'the time is now ripe for a suitable reconstruction of the ground floor.' *The Geisha*, which is advertised on the bus, was playing in 1906 at Daly's. The misty view looks north up Haverstock Hill, a year before Chalk Farm tube station opened. Built by the Charing Cross, Euston and Hampstead Railway, and known as the Hampstead Tube, it now forms part of the Northern Line.

FOLLOWING A REBUILD after a fire in 1985, the pub was replaced by commercial premises. Until recently, the area in front was still a bus terminus. Chalk Farm tube station is in the distinctive style adopted by Leslie Green for Northern line stations of the period. A convenient second exit onto Haverstock Hill has been closed. The name first proposed was 'Adelaide Road Station', as a Chalk Farm railway station already existed a short walk away on Regent's Park Road.

BEDDALL'S STORE, KENTISH TOWN ROAD

BEDDALL'S STOOD ON the corner with Holmes Road and is pictured on the right soon after rebuilding in 1900. This was one of the largest drapery businesses in the neighbourhood, also briefly trading from Nos 303-305. Like his neighbours the Daniel brothers (who were also drapers), Herbert Beddall was the son of an Essex farmer. He began trading in Kentish Town in around 1874 with just one shop, No. 293, which he took over from Messrs Manning. He later ran the business with his son John and appears to have retired in around 1910. The crowded window displays are typical of the period.

BEDDALL'S CLOSED IN 1922. The building was then split to provide retail space for Montague Burton the tailor's, as well as a costumier's and a Lyon's tearoom. It has since been redeveloped as shops, with office space above. The Electric Alhambra cinema opened at Nos 303-305 in February 1911 with seating for 500 patrons; its entrance in Holmes Road provided separate access to the tearoom. It shut in 1918, and in 1932, both properties were redeveloped as a Marks & Spencer store, which closed in 1981.

C. & A. DANIELS,
KENTISH TOWN ROAD

C. & A. DANIELS, 207-211a Kentish Town Road, in 1903. In 1865 Charles and Alfred started their draper's business in a single shop, and by the First World War the company had expanded into eleven of the shops between Prince of Wales Road and Anglers Lane. A third brother, Edward, also worked in the business. The parents of author V.S. Pritchett met at the store in the 1890s; he was a shopwalker, she a milliner. 'She could put a ugly hat on a grumbling woman, give a twist, snatch a feather or a bunch of cherries and so dazzle the customer with chatter and her smiles.' The male employees 'lived over the shop', where working hours were 8 a.m. to 8 p.m. on weekdays – and to 11 p.m. on Saturday! The living-in system was much disliked, and a strike at Daniels' involving twenty-four shop assistants lasted sixteen weeks before it was agreed to end the system.

BOMB DAMAGE DURING the Second World War prompted an employee to write this ode: 'Hitler tried for our destruction/

By dropping bombs in our direction./ He'll not break our resolution,/ Daniels still gives satisfaction.' In 1952, the shop celebrated its eighty-seventh anniversary (a strange date to choose) when the Beverley Sisters, a popular singing trio, signed their latest record in Daniels' new TV department. There was a knitting competition and every hundredth customer was offered a free perm. Daniels remained a family concern but didn't keep up with the times: it was 'unbelievably old-fashioned', according to one assistant. The business was sold in 1954, finally closing in 1963. Today, the appearance of the upper stories is much the same as in Daniels' day, with new shop fronts at street level.

SALMON & GLUCKSTEIN, KENTISH TOWN ROAD

IN 1903, ADVERTISEMENTS in Salmon and Gluckstein's Kentish Town shop windows correctly claimed the firm to be the 'largest tobacconists in the world' with 140 shops. But this was not their only business. Family members were co-founders of J. Lyons and Co., which opened teashops up and down the country (there was one close by, in the old Beddall's

premises). They also built the Trocadero in London's West End and, at its peak, Lyons was Europe's largest food producer. The tobacconist's elaborate window display was typical of the time and matched by David Levy, the fruiterer next door at No. 199.

No. 199 HAD become part of the Daniels' drapery empire by 1913. Salmon and Gluckstein had also gone, replaced that year by the Palace, later the Gaumont cinema. The shop site was used as the entry to the cinema, which opened its doors at No. 197 Kentish Town Road on 8 December. The main building lay behind the shops, reaching as far as Prince of Wales Road, where its end wall still stands. The cinema closed in 1959. Today an NHS facility is based at No. 197 and the building appears to have been completely rebuilt. No. 199 forms part of a larger supermarket.

J. SAINSBURY,
KENTISH TOWN ROAD

J. SAINSBURY'S KENTISH Town shop in 1955, soon after it had opened. This store replaced another at Nos 194-196, which shut the same year. It was devoted to a new shopping concept for

the UK: that of self service. Management knew that counter service was both labour intensive and time consuming. After the Second World War, building restrictions that favoured redeveloping bomb sites helped the developers of this site: Nos 230-254 had all been bomb-damaged. The shop was a complete rebuild, and a wraparound glass frontage gave Kentish Town shoppers an uninterrupted view of the interior with its many checkouts. Note the large number of pushchairs and infants left unattended outside. This was one of three Sainsbury's on the High Road, all now closed.

(Photograph reproduced with kind permission of The Sainsbury Archive, Museum of London Docklands, Kentish Town Road.)

SAINSBURY'S HAD A long history in Kentish Town, opening their second store at No. 159 Queens Crescent in 1873; the business began in central London, with a shop in Drury Lane. The company now trades locally from its large supermarket on Camden Road, adjacent to St Michael's church. This Sainsbury's branch shut in 1968. Minus its 1955 glass frontage, the building currently remains a supermarket.

CAMDEN ROAD STATION

THIS SHOWS CAMDEN Road station on the Midland Railway line. The station opened in 1868, replacing two villas on the main road. The platforms were downstairs, in a deep cutting behind the station building. Situated on the corner of Sandall and Camden Roads, this station was convenient for pupils of North London Collegiate School for Girls, the substantial building in the background. In 1870, Thomas Bowman, the Camden Town shop owner, sold the North London Collegiate a two-storey warehouse in Sandall Road. This was converted and extended, and the school opened in 1879. A further extension, which included the tower, opened in 1908.

TO BEGIN WITH, the station was well used: in 1872 over a quarter of a million tickets were issued. But passenger numbers fell as road transport expanded. The station closed in January 1916, the victim of declining passenger numbers and wartime economies. The building eventually became a petrol station, but steps to the platform level remained in the 1960s. Today, the garage has been replaced by a motor-car salesroom and service centre. In January 1941, bombs badly damaged the North London Collegiate buildings. As the school had already moved to Edgware, the Camden School for Girls agreed to take over the site, moving into the repaired buildings in 1956. More classrooms and an assembly hall were added in the mid-1960s. Famous old girls include the actresses Emma Thompson and Jodhi May, the film director Beeban Kidron, the author Deborah Moggach and Julia Donaldson, creator of the 'Gruffalo'.

CAMDEN LOCK
AND THE CHALK FARM
ROAD BRIDGE

THE PHOTOGRAPH BELOW looks east and was taken during rebuilding of the Chalk Farm Road Bridge and Hampstead Road Lock (better known as Camden Lock) on the Regent's Canal, which took place from 1876 to 1877. The original 1815 brick bridge was collapsing under increased road

traffic and only allowed one canal boat through at a time. The new bridge opened in May 1877. While it attracted general praise, the St Pancras vestry surveyor was critical, describing its 'intense ugliness'. For him, the problem lay with the bridge's peculiar construction; in particular increasing the span over the canal from 20 to 50ft meant using girders, parts of which projected above the level of the road, dividing it in two. Until the railways took over, transporting goods by canal helped local industry to prosper: Pickford the carriers, the many piano businesses, and, in particular, Gilbey's wine and spirits merchant, who had extensive premises nearby.

LOOKING UNDER THE Chalk Farm Road Bridge towards Hawley lock. One of the canal boats used for pleasure trips is moored on the right. On the left, two stones have been set into the wall at either end of the bridge. One is the key or 'guilders' stone of the 1815 bridge. The second is a corner stone, showing the date of the rebuild and the names of the St Pancras officials involved. The tow path continues past another market, which occupies space once the preserve of car repair shops and scrap merchants. It has recently reopened following a fire in 2008; the blaze also damaged properties on Castlehaven and Chalk Farm Roads. Currently there is a proposal to redevelop this area alongside the canal. This would bring yet more people to the area and has lead to discussions about reopening the nearby South Kentish Town tube station.

CAMDEN TOWN STATION
ON CAMDEN ROAD

THE PHOTOGRAPH BELOW looks northeast up Camden Road towards Camden Town station on the North London Railway (now London Overground Silverlink), *c.* 1905. Intended as a link from Chalk Farm to the docks at Poplar via Bow, the railway opened in 1850. The first station was a small wooden building at the end of the bridge but on the other side of Camden Road. In 1864,

a boiler explosion caused the engine of a stationary train to plunge off the bridge into Randolph Street below. The fireman died and local property was damaged, but the railway was largely unaffected. In less than two hours, trains began running again! The present station was relocated following line widening. Designed on a grand scale by Edwin Horne, it opened on 7 December 1870. Trains ran west to Kew and Richmond or east to Poplar, with a 14-minute service to the City at Broad Street.

ALTHOUGH THE STATION was renamed Camden Road in 1950, today the old name is still displayed at roof level. This is the only surviving station by Edwin Horne on the North London Line, and the interior has been much altered. The ornamental ironwork is also missing. From 1979 trains began running to North Woolwich and the Broad Street extension was closed in June 1986. Today the line terminates at Stratford.

CAMDEN TOWN UNDERGROUND STATION

THIS PHOTOGRAPH BELOW shows the site of Camden Town Underground station in about 1903. The remarkable building on the left was nicknamed the 'cows' cathedral' by locals, because of its elaborate gothic exterior. Claimed to be established in 1790 by farmer Thomas Brown, the dairy was certainly here from 1822. The cows grazed on the Kentish Town fields before they were built over, and were later kept in brick sheds behind the dairy. The immaculate house with its whitened steps was the Brown's family home. Thomas was succeeded by son Charles; then, in 1881, Charles' widow, Mary Ann, took over, describing herself as a dairywoman and employing ten men. The property was purchased – to become the site of the underground station – and in December 1903 the dairy moved to Parkway. Opened in 1907, the tube station shares a common design with others in the neighbourhood, all by Leslie Green.

TODAY'S UNDERGROUND STATION sits behind the dairy site, which is now a bank, following significant rebuilding after suffering bomb damage in 1940. Note the two relief panels with a medical and scientific theme. The station is the entry point every year for millions of tourists visiting the area's many markets, shops and restaurants. The station struggles with the huge numbers of passengers, and as part of a larger redevelopment, involving all the properties north to Buck Street, its facilities were to be modernised. This plan would have meant demolishing a popular music venue, the Electric Ballroom, as well as the open-air 'Camden Market' opposite Inverness Street. U2, Madness, The Clash and The Smiths have all played at the Electric Ballroom and recent performers have included The Killers and Paul McCartney. Currently the redevelopment plans have been refused and the future of the station remains undecided.

THE ROUNDHOUSE,
CHALK FARM

THE INTERIOR OF the Roundhouse in 1847 (below), soon after opening. The functional, circular design by Robert Benson Dockray was deliberate: it was to accommodate a central turntable for moving engines to bays, twenty-three in all. Beneath each bay was an inspection pit. But it was soon made redundant, due to increased engine size. By the early 1860s, the building was a store for potatoes and corn, and in 1869 it was leased to Gilbey's as a bonded gin store. In 1846 a fight broke out between two groups of labourers: Irish (working near

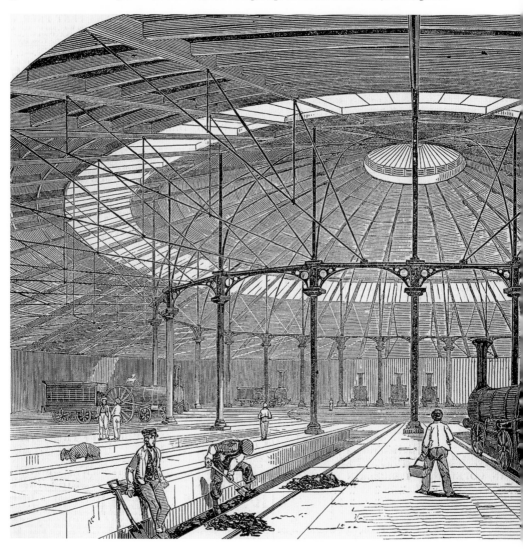

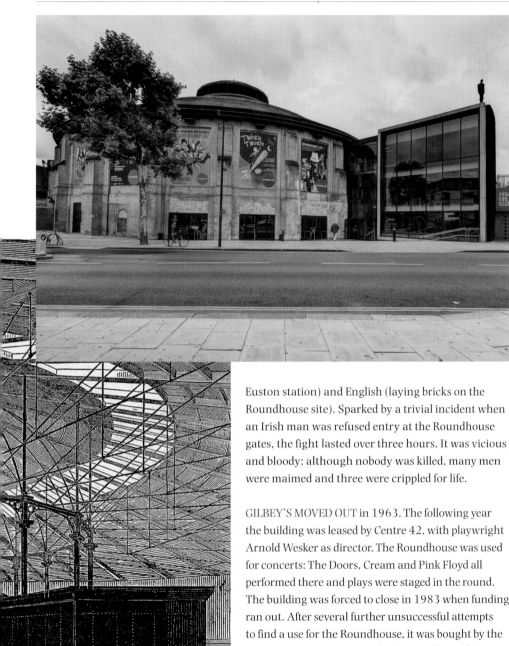

Euston station) and English (laying bricks on the Roundhouse site). Sparked by a trivial incident when an Irish man was refused entry at the Roundhouse gates, the fight lasted over three hours. It was vicious and bloody: although nobody was killed, many men were maimed and three were crippled for life.

GILBEY'S MOVED OUT in 1963. The following year the building was leased by Centre 42, with playwright Arnold Wesker as director. The Roundhouse was used for concerts: The Doors, Cream and Pink Floyd all performed there and plays were staged in the round. The building was forced to close in 1983 when funding ran out. After several further unsuccessful attempts to find a use for the Roundhouse, it was bought by the Norman Trust in 1996, with the aim of providing a creative centre for young people. The interior of the Grade II listed building has been restored and adapted – at a cost of £30 million – and much of the original ironwork is on display. A performance space, café and meeting spaces have all been provided. The figure on the roof is by the well-known sculptor Antony Gormley.

CHALK FARM ROAD
AND THE CANAL BRIDGE

THE PHOTOGRAPH ON the right looks north over the bridge in about 1905, showing the girder dividing the road after the bridge was rebuilt. Camden Lock is to the left, and at this point both banks of the canal were lined with prosperous commercial premises. Although less busy than Camden High Street, Chalk Farm Road was also an important shopping street. The photograph shows Henry Roberts, tailor, at No. 1, the first shop beyond the bridge. Next came Lilley & Skinner's boot makers at Nos 2 and 3, the Horseshoe coffee and dining rooms at No. 6, and the Carnarvon Castle public house near the corner with Castlehaven Road. The horse bus was on its way to Victoria, with a happy family – dad, mum and baby – up top.

THE AWKWARD ROAD division has been removed and traffic is one way. Today, this is the hub of a busy tourist area based in and around Camden Lock. The Lock and main market are to the left. On the right beyond the bridge, hoardings enclose shops and premises damaged by the 2008 fire. This started around 7.30 p.m. on the 9 February, in the market area behind the houses. Apparently the cause was a banned liquid petroleum gas heater which set fire to material, but fortunately no one was hurt. The flames also gutted the Hawley Arms in Castlehaven Road, another popular live music venue and favourite of the late Amy Winehouse. The pub has since reopened. This bridge is crossed by millions of people every year, in search of bargains, food and entertainment.

Other titles published by The History Press

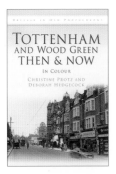

Tottenham & Wood Green Then & Now
CHRIS PROTZ & DEBORAH HEDGECOCK

The Tottenham and Wood Green area has seen dramatic changes over the decades. Its rural villages, farms and market gardens have now been absorbed into the bustle of Greater London and the area has left its rural days behind. This selection of archive images, placed alongside beautiful modern photography of Tottenham's streets today, capture these fascinating transformations, and show how much has changed, how much has stayed the same, and the ways in which the old still influences the new.

978 0 7524 6328 5

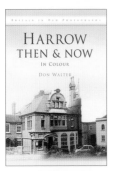

Harrow Then & Now
DON WALTER

Modern Harrow has changed both a huge amount and surprisingly little over the last 100 years, due both to population growth and the clever actions of far-sighted town administrators of decades past. Placing these archive images alongside beautiful modern photography of the same views today and fascinating informative captions, *Harrow Then & Now* takes us on a tour of the changing face of this historic area, from the modern central streets to the beautifully preserved historic school in Harrow on the Hill.

978 0 7524 6327 8

London's Disasters: from Boudicca to the Banking Crisis
JOHN WITHINGTON

London has been hit by wave upon wave of destruction. This fascinating and unique book tells the story of over 2,000 years of disaster from fire, water, disease, pollution, accident, storm, riot, terrorism and enemy action. It chronicles well-known episodes like the Great Plague of 1655 and the Blitz, as well as lesser-known events such as whirlwinds and earthquakes. *London's Disasters* ultimately celebrates the spirit of its people who have risen above it all and for whom London is one of the greatest cities on earth.

978 0 7524 5747 5

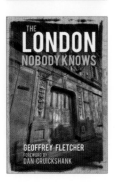

The London Nobody Knows
GEOFFREY FLETCHER

Geoffrey Fletcher's off-beat portrayal of London does not focus on the big landmarks, but rather 'the tawdry, extravagant and eccentric'. His descriptions will transport you to an art nouveau pub, a Victorian music hall, a Hawksmoor church and even a public toilet in Holborn in which the attendant kept goldfish in the cisterns. Drawn to the corners where 'the kids swarm like ants and there are dogs everywhere', Fletcher will take you to parts of the city where few outsiders venture.

978 0 7524 6199 1

Visit our website and discover thousands of other History Press books.

www.thehistorypress.co.uk

The History Press